I0449399

PARTITION

Looking at the World Structured by Human Rights and Non-Lethality

MICHAEL LAPAJENKO

authorHOUSE®

AuthorHouse™
1663 Liberty Drive
Bloomington, IN 47403
www.authorhouse.com
Phone: 1 (800) 839-8640

© 2016 Michael Lapajenko. All rights reserved.

No part of this book may be reproduced, stored in a retrieval system, or transmitted by any means without the written permission of the author.

Published by AuthorHouse   12/06/2016

ISBN: 978-1-5246-5178-7 (sc)
ISBN: 978-1-5246-5177-0 (e)

Print information available on the last page.

Any people depicted in stock imagery provided by Thinkstock are models, and such images are being used for illustrative purposes only. Certain stock imagery © Thinkstock.

This book is printed on acid-free paper.

Because of the dynamic nature of the Internet, any web addresses or links contained in this book may have changed since publication and may no longer be valid. The views expressed in this work are solely those of the author and do not necessarily reflect the views of the publisher, and the publisher hereby disclaims any responsibility for them.

TABLE OF CONTENTS

INTRODUCTION

Countries are obsessed with unilateralism and consumed by internal affairs. A plan that leads to the creation of a united planet by way of voluntary compliance is needed. Even though things are getting better. Domestic perceptions of US leadership in the world are on the decline, hence the rise of Teabag movement and Donald Trump. The argument here is it is not about who has the most successful economic system or who has the stronger leader. The US has been the world's whipping boy for long enough. The US is an example of what a free society can achieve. It is time for the US to take the superpower target off its back. Instead of being the only superpower in the world it can go back to roots of the US birth, it was against kings. Are kings the superpowers of the past? Political managers in the world mistakenly took focus off ideology and emphasized economics. The US became the source, wrongly, of the world's problems. All the country was doing was providing land for the evolution of freedom. It has not been the smoothest of rides, just ask the Native Americans, the African Americans (thought: if a black goes to Africa does that make him an American African?) the Asian Americans, or Latino Americans. All possess a number of unresolved issues. Most issues stem from being distracted by economics and not ideology.

The ideology of control, disguised as nationalism, has created nationalistic movements in all countries emphasized by blocking out immigrants. Lost in this humanitarian effort of permitting or encouraging the free movement of all people to move away from countries practicing the ideology of control.

Under it all is the ideology of nationalism. Some think nationalism is just national pride. Although national pride is important to have nationalism is like that saying, "You can't see the forest because of the trees." Nationalism leads to the blindness of not seeing the welfare of a country without controls.

Nationalism also narrows the view of patriotism. Patriotism is not limited to the affairs of a single country, but the affairs and the direction of all humanity. Every country has a role for patriotism, but some countries are at the vanguard. The US is one of those, not because of its economic standing but its ability to introduce new ideas of freedom.

A new paradigm will emerge from the chaos and give people a psychological perspective on humanity and connections to other people. We will be entering into the "Age of Unity" by way of a new paradigm. The new paradigm will occur by way of new technology.

Unity is an ideology of connection and freedom. Every society is connected and helps to create a community of freedom. Basically, it is an arena where unilateral objectives are cast aside and the interests of the free community dominate. If something occurs in another region of the world it affects all others in the community. This has given rise to the theory of the butterfly effect. For instance an action such as increasing oil prices can be felt around the world. The rest of the world puts on economic blinders, where economics take priority over what is right or wrong, as many of these actions are just camouflaged military adventures. This ignites a series of counteractions and reactions to fuel a regional arms race. These actions are usually current prejudices, regional paranoia and military possibilities. Military adventures furnish the ability to occupy by force, disgard responsibility, and dismiss global equality and unity. Military adventures are solutions founded in deterrence, nationalism and brutal violence. They are motivated by self-interest.

Human rights are part of military adventures since it enables the country conducting the adventure to involuntarily impose their interpretation of human rights on occupied lands. Every country has their own definition of human rights, Russia believes in further restricting freedoms and imposing Soviet-style control on territory and people. The People's Republic of China (PRC) believes an elite class that rejects all dissent can only determine the answer. The struggle between freedom and repression has been an element of every struggle for people. For instance the American Revolution, the

French Revolution, the French and Indian Wars, the War between States, the Indian liberation wars, World War One, World War Two, the French Indochina War, Iran and Iraq, many examples are distributed throughout history. Not every struggle has resulted in the victory of freedom.

The definition of human rights varies with each country because the legal structures within each country are different. Legal structures are as numerous as countries. So many have different definitions for the same thing. A common legal structure is needed, not exactly the same, but customized to each country. Customized to allow all people to reach their full human potential. Human rights are universal. No country has a definite grip on it, so in 1948 countries from every region in the world signed the United Nations Universal Declaration of Human Rights to establish a common definition for all. When the various UN representatives returned to their respective countries, and as nationalism took precedence, the definitions changed. The representatives found their countries involved in different stages of repressive and freedom-encouraging behavior.

Human rights depended on a country's behavior and economic status it had set for itself. International recognition is linked to a country's economic rating. Currently, membership in various organizations is determined by economics. Economics justifies overlooking human rights. Recognition is based on economic strength not moral character. Economics determines the measure of a country, human rights has become a secondary consideration.

UN Habitat estimates 1 in 6 people are in poverty, that means 1 in 6 people globally will experience some sort of run-in with human rights. Since poorer people tend to be in areas where many violations are commonplace their chances are higher than the rest of the population infrastructure to be involved in violations.

Complexity is removed if human rights analysis of each country is conducted to determine the degrees of control or degrees of freedom. The extreme views of repression involve torture, executions, disappearances, and/ or extreme methods of population control. While repressive countries seek to control their people; free countries do not.

If you analyze each country it clearly reveals a hierarchy of countries that can be broken to form two separate political blocs. This distinction also indicates which countries can be allies and those that cannot. Countries can only be allies if they belong to the same political ideology. Meaning that a controlling country cannot be allied with a free country. This jeopardizes many relationships that countries have forged. The US and the PRC, the US and Azerbaijan, are some of the relationships. Although countries, like Azerbaijan, can be labeled with human rights violations and be called controlling, they are not one of the extreme controlling countries in the world.

As a member of the Free World, a status that is determined by unanimous consent from all countries in the Free World, after they convert to being free from being a controlling country. The recognition comes with a complete development package and involvement in an international security alliance. Their volunteer efforts would merge with other free countries to form a political system protected by volunteers. Their protection would be non-lethal.

Partition into two major ideologies in the world would remove many of the complexities of international relations—East or West, North or South, developed or undeveloped. The ideologies are degrees of freedom (laxity) and degrees of repression (control). We should not polarize countries as communist or capitalist. We should not describe countries by economic system; this assessment ignores behaviors like nationalism and contributes to the mistaken belief that includes all countries. We should be using a new and different approach avoiding nation-state chest pounding or economic myopia. Under this approach nationalistic terms are put aside and the world is considered as a holistic unit—an all-encompassing world-view and unifying strategies. The basis is the similarity of the human condition and internationally agreed upon human rights.

With a new paradigm, ideals take precedence. Ideology must become the foundation for all actions. Genome sequencing determined 99.9% of everybody are basically the same, and unify can only happen we become a single group loyal to each other. Do not impose colonialism, territorial expansion or any other means to constrict human evolution. Bring all cultures that were separated, together again.

Unity will come with a new paradigm. A new paradigm will require an assessment of every county for their degree of freedom (laxity) and repression (control). A free world begins with validating a country's level of domestic and foreign behavior. On a country level, the amount of restriction indicates the level of repression in a country. A group that maintains the Political Terror Survey for the US State Department would be a good place to start the assessment.

Freedom is unhindered personal physical space, unbound mental tolerance, and the unrestricted ability to pursue spirituality. Repression is control of the physical, mental, and spiritual elements of a person.

Humanity's conflict for freedom is never over. A new view of humanity and the use of military force must occur to provide leadership for the Free World. The first step is to use a holistic strategy to integrate all people of the world and not categorize people by individual and separate cultures such as Chinese, Latino, black, white, or any number of nation-state derivatives. Census data concerning ethnic background must be thrown out in all free countries. We are not a quilt; we are, if we pursue this analogy, a blanket. (Using a divisive quilt approach is where 6% of people are Asian, 61% white, 12% black, and 18% Hispanic, according to 2015 data by the Kaiser Family Foundation.) These strategies are isolationist, unilateral, and focused on differences. Instead of focusing on similarities.

Incorporating multiculturalism into country analysis only institutionalizes differences. Multiculturalism, like nationalism and unilateralism, is a tool to further divide us and create suspicion. It narrows the focus to individual interests vice those of the whole. (The former British Prime Minister Mr. Cameroon pointed this out in 2011 about multiculturalism during a speech in Munich, Germany to indicate there are two general philosophies in the world; to be repressive {controlling} or to be free. The UK and the rest of the Free World encourage freedom and others do not.) People were told about the foundation for unity through freedom.

A country that has a culture of repression and control cannot have one of its individuals be immediately integrated into a free society. It's like trying to immediately integrate a peacock into a herd of cows. Though the integration can be done gradually and locally, oversight must be the responsibility of the community and generational inhabitants to ensure there's no backslide into terrorism.

The forces of freedom have always been in conflicts with the forces of repression/control. These have been portrayed as capitalist vs. communists, liberators vs. fascists, unions vs. management, poor vs. rich, etc. The creation of armies and organized warfare, led to physical entities structured in a conflict with each other. Every recorded conflict has been a continuation of this ideological struggle. These conflicts include the Boxer Rebellion, the Bolshevik Revolution, the French Revolution, the American Revolution, World War II, and the Cold War, all humanity's conflicts. Freedom has always been the goal of one side and repression is the goal of the other.

One of the greatest distracters is economic theory. Issues are deemed complex because ideology is ignored and the economic structure of a repressive country is assumed to be equal to that of a free country, regardless of questionable issues. Each country is completely different. A central control economy is not the same as one that is involved in free trade. Because of the popularity for the study of economics, ideology has become a secondary consideration. Economics contributes to the global financial mess and shows the arrogance of humanity as it tries to define the operations of people. A report in the Washington Post in 1987 used economics to promote trends in politics and the growth of jobs until 2010, but no mention of ideology. Because economics has been popularly accepted on the same lines as math its credibility borders on sacrosanct. Yet modern events have proven it is wrong. Economic predictions in the 80s implied Japan would be dominant economic force in the world. Once again they were wrong. Brazil, Russia, India, and China (BRIC) New world leaders? Wrong. Economics is just an attempt to establish control over the social and political realms. Economics is about the same as microscopic navel gazing. It takes focus away from goals and focuses on immediate returns. In other words it distracts.

Today, the forces of freedom, those with long-term goals, continue the battle with repression. Life is not about economics or output; it is and always will be about the quality of long-term life as defined by freedom and human rights. Ultimately, all politics is about freedom and repression. Only analyzing economic factors ignores other factors of life, like morality, honesty, etc.

An incentive to convert to freedom is by becoming an equal modern country and economic superpower able to trade modern, quality products and services with other free regional members. Modernization should not be a tedious process of step-by-step economic development, but tied to ideological commitments. It should be the bedrock of an international community. If a country remains repressive then they will remain locked on the continuous path of economic development. Those that are closer to the ideology of freedom and more lax will not. A better world is available by converting to freedom and joining the community of free countries.

The world does not need a military superpower. Military superpowers pursue unilateral perspectives in economic, political and world affairs. Besides one country should not be isolated as the world's caretaker— it should be a shared responsibility of a united bloc of countries. In previous centuries the dominance of a single country reflected the anointing of a top dog, basically a king of all countries. This brought us colonialism, exploitation, occupation, slavery and other behavior married to unilateral interests and no concern for the welfare of all people. In future centuries a single ideology unites all countries without unilateral interests. Any direct action to repel and defeat repression is a group concern of the entire Free World. Any action will be conducted with collective international security. A new form of security becomes necessary. Collective international security allows free countries to enter into a multi-country alliance. The basis of a new defense system refrains from killing and provides security.

Security brings forth a non-lethal alliance of everyone. Countries that are part of this alliance no longer have to integrate large, costly weapon systems into their yearly defense budgets instead they can put more funds towards the welfare of their citizens. In the US, the defense budget will be reduced as collective security becomes a shared concern of the entire Free World. Countries will be able to prove that people are the most valuable resource—not things or economic assets. Collective security protects regional markets for the Free World's goods. It does not protect any repressive products or repressive lands.

Country financial reduction occurs with not maintaining consulates, diplomatic outposts or embassies in dangerous repressive countries. Since diplomatic relations will be premised on similar philosophical belief, more relation will be geared to cooperative relations not competitive.

Freedom will establish three free markets The advantage of a regional market place is quick manufacturer response, an intuitive understanding and awareness of the market, lower marketing costs, downtimes, regional employment opportunities, and an appreciation for regional environmental concerns. A stream of entrepreneurial possibilities emerges from a regional approach to business. This approach paves the way for new technologies to enter the region and provides a need for developing employment and financial stability.

Gaining individual sovereignty means adhering to international standards of behavior for freedom and becoming part of the bloc. Society based on confining economic theories only confuses people and clouds perspective.

A repressive society is a society to be leery about. Repressive and controlling regimes use any weapons that are available in their fight against freedom. Terrorism is one of those weapons. Terrorism is mistakenly viewed as a material confrontation and political manipulation. It is really a tool for ideological confrontation and it is method of psychological warfare for persuasion. A material fight against terrorism without attacking its psychological roots is just attacking a symptom. The real culprit is the battle against repression. Confronting terrorism begins by isolating repressive traits as they relate to elements of freedom, hence country assessments.

Terrorism is not inevitable. It can be successfully confronted and controlled. The present way of dealing with terrorism is primarily on reaction and hope. Reaction when it does happen and hope that it will not. Confronting terrorism begins with the understanding that it just a repressive action initiated by a repressive state or organization in an effort to further spread repression. Remove all the psychological factors that foster terrorism and you have a society ready for conversion—such as becoming a developed country. As society imposes further controls on itself as it becomes more repressive. This results in more Transportation Security Agency (TSA) controls on the flying public, more metal detectors, more police, more weapon sales, etc.

Terrorism is not an action all by itself. Terrorism is a tool of repression. The Lockerbie bombing in 1988, the USS Cole attack in 2000, the Spanish bombing in 2004, the British subway bombings in 2005, or the Mumbai attack in 2008 were tools for repression—specific organizations supporting a specific material cause. If this is recognized, then the source for control and manipulation can be identified. Action should be taken against the sources of repression. Once recognized as such, new non-lethal counterterrorist tactics can be designed to confront it. Showing progress against repression and its allies that use terrorism can be done by addressing the source of repression.

The struggle for freedom against repression continues. In present times, the forces of freedom risk becoming tools of repression. Countries may think they are still on the side of good, but unwittingly they become an instrument of repression by becoming coercive and controlling in countering repression. This occurs when a country thinks it is to doing good, but adopts the ways of repression. Israel is a good candidate for this...so is the TSA... or Russia and Ukraine. Israel has erected an extensive control system to monitor Palestinians or other Arabs. Any relationship should be neutral. The War on Terror and the blind support for repressive allies, such as Pakistan, the People's Republic of China, Russia, Egypt, Japan and Israel, among others since they are more identifiable with repressive countries, the free countries of the world illustrate this. The foundation of freedom is clearly identified in the alliance of the Free World and the isolated countries of repression.

Each repressive country practices some form of repression. Japan maintains an informal apartheid system that treats non-Japanese as second-class citizens. Considering the various forms of repression, the ends do not justify the means. Usually, when the primary emphasis is placed on economics strategic planners disregardi long-term ideals, ideology, and concentrate on complex economic issues and nationalism while neglecting personal ethics such as public gatherings, citizen welfare, and freedom for all. They lose sight of the big picture and only focus on cash distribution to the regime.

THE FUTURE

A world of optimism and promise is waiting in the future. Future generations must look at past generations and invest in them—an investment in the development of new ideas and new businesses. After World War II returning veterans were given financial incentives to populate the suburbs and go to college. It is sad that the current generation benefitted the most from this government investment is not willing to invest in the current generations for the future. Their stinginess has blanketed the future in a dense fog. In such everything about the future is ominous. The future is perceived as a dark and threatening cloud of doom on the horizon.

Instead of viewing it negatively; the future is a sunrise of hope. As some say, "There's a light and the end of tunnel and it isn't an on-coming train." The present financial situation is expected to end; some say badly, some say not so much. Although pundits describe inevitable doom for the world, technical and social advances ensure prosperity and complete modernity for everyone. The world has become steadily safer—meaning it has become more peaceful. We no longer openly carry bows and swords. The children of today will be entering a world of non-lethal conflict resolution for international and domestic situations, new concepts of employment, technological sophistication, an improving environment, and unified families. The future will see social and technical improvements to society that tethers humanity to this lifestyle and frees it from the past.

Planes, cars, computers, space travel, medical breakthroughs, imaging technologies, GPS, and DVRs are just a partial list of innovations that are now a part of our everyday lives.

In the future, a holistic foreign strategy unites every country in the world and prevents separate coercive structures. The world should not be divided into separate structures with separate ideologies and different ideals. Separate coercive structures create different areas of cash-flow, they cannot be blended into one universal economy because of economic and ideological differences. An example, the economy of the United Kingdom is not the same as the People's Republic of China. Thus each has a different cash-flow infrastructure. An option for this is a holistic foreign strategy is complete freedom.

Countries of the world lack a standard for behavior. The world needs clearly definable categories of freedom and repression—categories that can be followed with a moral compass. Currently, there is no permanent measure. Countries and their rulers are given leeway to act like belligerent brats and claim internal affairs. Some execute and torture their citizens, conduct arbitrary arrests and detentions, or create a secret police force to oversee internal events. Other countries remain silent and ignore the events with international ramifications and only react afterwards. Rwanda, Libya, Congo, and Darfur are examples of this. Countries sit on the fence hoping that these places will not require foreign intervention. Unfortunately, the international community wants to avoid any foreign intervention, but sometimes a situation will force them. Some areas are undecided: Darfur, Afghanistan, Iraq, Iran, Syria, North Korea, and Georgia.

A globally agreed upon criterion should be established for freedom. The universal definition must consider basic human rights such as the levels of physical freedom, intellectual freedom, and spiritual freedom. Categorization by these factors determines membership and level of freedom in the Free World.

Countries unanimously say, in times of conflict, that it's too bad the United Nations does not have the power to enforce good behavior. When a crisis is over, countries do not vote to give the organization the power. The conflict in Darfur reveals the UN was becoming increasingly concerned, and did a gradual escalation of involvement.

Participation generally meant vocal outrage, but nothing intellectual to follow it up. Most countries would raise arguments about sovereignty and start waving the banner of internal affairs during the conflict, but get paralysis afterwards. Now that Sudan is not the subject of news worthy attention it is forgotten by most of the world.

Defining a conflict as a "good" or "bad" war is subjective and reserved for history books. The Mesopotamian Wars, the Crusades, and the Sino-Japanese War are examples of "good and bad" conflicts that played out this theme of freedom against repression, but their bearing on the future remains unknown.

No alliances are permanent. Some alliances are unable to withstand a thorough evaluation that clarifies their political positioning as repressive or free. Repressive and free countries cannot be on the same side. An example of this is the US and the PRC. Now if the US is on the way to being controlling then this is not a mismatch, but let's, for sake of argument, assume it is. By not having the same ideology, countries will, most likely, not believe in similar trade and labor practices—practices that cater to competition instead of cooperation. Cooperation begins the new paradigm. Competition contributes to unilateral controlling behavior and unilateral controlling ambitions.

If we stop using the future of film producers' and novelist's dystopia maybe people will stop having a negative spin on the future. We have the ability to set the tone of the future. Any visions that do not include the freedom versus repression ideals will become self-fulfilling negative prophecies of bad things to come. Is this the world we want to pass on?

Some of the common portrayals for the future include an uninhabited wasteland, the end of days, a world covered by the ocean, robots battling humans, slums, disease or plague, zombie apocalypse, cannibals and staggering overpopulation. Their message is, "The future will be bleak and dismal." These pictures of humankind do not reflect the threshold of technological and philosophical change that began at the end of the previous century with computerization, new health care possibilities, imaging technologies, nanotechnology, 3D printing, material manufacturing, etc.

There is positive growth and a new spiritual awakening that is not tied to religion or fiction. People are spiritually awakening to the planet and tapping into the ebbs and flows of the natural world. The rise in spirituality, cults, and some religions are good examples. Scientology and astronomy have helped to marshal in awakenings by creating doubt and further investigation into organized spirituality.

The future can unveil many new possibilities. Spiritual oneness as a possibility is to understand the vast network of connections, new innovations, and people to socially construct a planet that is free and unified. The world can be a place where people share a common operating philosophy—not a political philosophy such as democracy, but a common way of life that unleashes humankind's potential. In this new philosophy, children and families achieve their full potential by nourishing it. Under the present financial cloud, the future does not look promising, but are we locked into self-fulfilling prophecy?

A new understanding about the struggles of humanity and an increased awareness of the planet helps to define relationships to people, work and Earth. The question becomes, "Do we live to sustain ourselves or do we live to work?" Are we destined to be monetary workers or can we work for our and our family's survival?

Presently, the international community is not structured for unity; it is represented by a collection of ideologically opposed countries called the United Nations. The United Nations is anything but united. A widely diverse and ideologically polarized group of countries make up the international assembly. If you are a tract of land and you call yourself a country then you are welcomed to the UN. This results in philosophical differences and power grabs about how to govern countries. In the General Assembly anarchy, chaos, and gridlock prevail. This must change.

If countries of the world were divided along the polar axis of freedom and repression, these countries would be a catalyst for unity and the emergence of truly free regional markets. An ideologically bonded United Nations would revise itself so that only free countries were members. Membership would be contingent on unanimous approval from other free countries and the revised United Nations, itself.

It is easy to doubt with wars, terrorism, fundamentalist/radical idealism, the economy, the housing crisis, environmental demise, and other bleak outlooks. Most planners are used to projections based on a perfect set of circumstances and half the time they are wrong. As the author of Future Babble says "There's a fundamental psychological drive going on here, a basic human need for a sense of control and knowing what'll happen next, regardless of whether it actually happens or not." Basically people want a world of causes and results, but the world is full of unknowns. The world resembles a beginning than more of an end, it is not as bad as projections have made it seem. The initial decade of this century and the previous century have given humankind a wealth of innovations. Innovations that enable better communication, space technologies, air travel, advanced combat, and many more.

Although we have made many advances, we have made few gains in our ability to deal with conflict, the environment, crime, political ideologues and economic inflexibility. The future rests in our ability to successfully manage these issues. All of them have been overshadowed by one thing—economics, misguided lust for money, and maintaining the present infrastructure. Economics keeps focus narrowed to questionable projections and avoiding unknowns. People want things to be black and white—without shades of grey. They have forgotten the goal of every country should not focus on being the most prosperous or economically sound country, but should concentrate on complete laxity and having its citizens participating in everyday affairs—a holistic (whole body) strategy. The future should not be captive to incomplete models of increasing control that tell people how to live life. It is unfortunate that people overlook this in favor of economy-centric theories of the world, like the modern concept of national development. In the modern world, the United States and other countries of the Free World can reject this or lose credibility and forced to take off their economic blinders. For countries to handle any of these issues, they must all be placed in holistic (or possibly world-state) terms. Unity must become everyone's foreign policy.

ECONOMICS

Pigeon holing each country by assigning economic valuation cheapens ideological differences and throws all countries on the heap called sameness. Assigning and limiting a country's importance by its degree of economic success is a dangerous mistake. Using economic analysis to project past reasoning into the future indicates a willingness to accept the current infrastructure with all of its blemishes. The U.S.'s budget deficit of $19T and the current debt strategies are examples of rigid economic reasoning and forecasting, which creates debt limits and an unwillingness to invest in present society and its people.

Economic standing does not rate a country; behavior does. This economic determination makes it difficult for authoritarian and free countries to be allies. In a world divided into regions of freedom and control there is no "two-state" proposals. Proposals like Israel and the Palestinians or Taiwan and the PRC, are unrealistic because they disregard the ideological foundation of there only being one world, a free world. There is no peaceful coexistence between any countries of the free and repressed worlds only armed standoff. The Japanese emphasized this on going conflict to the US and the rest of the Free World with economic differences in the 80s and now the PRC is attempting to best the Free World using economic warfare. At the core of all countries can be assessed as free or controlling this determination indicates whether they can cohabitate.

If economic reasoning is used to justify a material way of life, then crime will prosper. People use economics to place monetary importance on things in life. Once materialism becomes the mindset, people begin collecting things to give meaning to their existence, hence the saying, "He who has the most toys when they die—wins." Materialism attracts crime. This is not meant to be a study about the causation of crime, but an identification of potential targets. The relationship between crime and economics has been the subject of study for many years. Causation has been based on employment, geographies, control, or culture, etc.

It is important to realize that crime is a nesting and opportunistic behavior that tries to increase economic status by the accumulation of wealth. Criminals target wealth or materialism and those that have it flaunt it in effort to obtain it or advertise their status. Issues of good or bad are ignored because of materialism and the attraction it creates for criminals, like blood in the water for sharks, is similar. On a national level, economics only entice people to become materialistic and open the door to crime such as the emergence of billion dollar Ponsi scandals on Wall Street, vanishing retirement accounts, and excessive speculation. On an international level, it encourages military adventurism, gangster behavior on the national level. In both it encourages speculation.

Established economic models have distinct cash flows, but say nothing about ideology. They determine wealth distribution, but not mental disposition. If a country is controlling the cash it usually flows to the regime, but little flows to the people. This is why most authoritarian rulers are well to do. So average people suffer while the regime gets richer. Take North Korea the rulers of the country dined lavishly while their subjects starved and ate tree bark. This is happening in many of the repressive countries as they struggle with the financial crisis in economic terms. They suffer famines, epidemics, and a very hard life. In Ethiopia mismanagement contributed to one of the world's worst droughts and in Zimbabwe government mismanagement has turned the country that could have been the breadbasket for all of Africa to one that cannot produce enough for its citizens. Take, as additional examples, events in Sudan or Burma. The rulers do not share the same economic hardships of the citizens.

If humanity wishes to survive, all people and every country must accept freedom. Freedom is alien to economics—even though it is used in welfare calculations, freedom usually is a second-hand concern. If there is an economic theory for a country, it should be understanding the ideological position aids in making sense of the cash flow. Just follow the money. Citizen participation and the level of freedom identify the various influences within a country and their impact on unity and the money trails. Foremost, a country's importance is not the based solely on the measure of economics; it is a combination of other factors beyond cash flow.

Money in the present financial environment has been declining. The global financial situation is premised on keeping present structures intact and putting the burden on others.

Economics is money. Each government spends some of its budget on social welfare and defense. The priority determines country's ideological leaning and the amount of spending in each category. Most repressive regimes will spend more strengthening their defense capabilities and control than providing comfort for their citizens. Most countries have an outlook that is unilateral not multilateral. Defense based on deterrence generates armed stand offs and creates a region for spiraling defense costs. In the future a member of the Free World should share the financial burden of defense with other free countries and be in an organization for collective security.

Every country that is a part of the Free World must be united against all forms of repression. Countries have multilateral concerns such water rights, transportation, refugees, etc. Collective security provides options for rooting out repression and addressing these matters. Unity and collective security helps the Free World. There will be no need to maintain expensive defense or law enforcement forces and ordinance if the Free World maintains a collective, multilateral approach. If one disregards the clarity of hindsight, the choice of maintaining a social safety net or upgrading its war fighting machinery is a problem that faces every country. The future will be one that is dedicated countries that wish to allocate the majority of their national budgets to social efforts. A defense system needs to be institutionalized that ensures international security. National protection should naturally come from this international entity by providing the entire Free World collective security. Instead of each country having to spend billions on its own defense it will fall under the umbrella of collective security. It will not be the same umbrella that was put up for deterrence, where strength and unilateralism is acceptable. It will be an umbrella that covers countries that believe in voluntary compliance and the virtues of freedom.

Defense will not be based on the possession of expensive systems or deterrence theories. It will be based on the principles of multilateralism and adherence to the ideals of complete freedom. A country will not have to depend on massive amounts of duplicated platforms like tanks and fighter aircraft. The emphasis for defense will be on collective security, non-lethality, and cost sharing. Defense will not be the responsibility of one country it will be the responsibility of all free countries for the protection of the entire bloc. It will be many against one.

Multilateralism and unity will initiate a new UN to fill the role as a central assemblage point for actions to defend the Free World. Its primary concern is to ensure any actions by Free World forces are non-lethal and clearly distinguishable from actions by repressed forces.

NON-LETHALITY

Critical to any global strategy is non-lethal technology. Non-lethal technology is a science that distinguishes the good guys from the bad guys. It presents a clear dividing line for the interpretation of power. It points out power is anything but coercion. No arm-twisting to get a desired out come. Non-lethal technology is the evolution of warfare and a total disengagement from an accepted defense theory—deterrence. The ability to assess each country by human rights requires the integration of biology and technology for conflict resolution. Unlike deterrence a new non-lethal defense theory does not push anyone into compliance; their actions are completely voluntary.

Right now the feasibility of many non-lethal concepts are being tested. Capability of non-lethal technology and applications is accepted, but size, weight and power sources have received an unwelcomed hello. It is hoped that most new non-lethal technologies will develop like blue-ray players/recorders, ipods, ipads and laptops, high at first but slowly coming down in price and an increase in capability.

Non-lethality is the next paradigm of change for humanity. It creates business locally, internationally and it stops the gradual disintegration of society's safety net. It can revive the manufacturing sector, stimulate an area that is some of the world's best—biotechnological, foster growth in employment sector, and lay a foundation for planning. Republicans believe there is more return in maintaining the current approach of high defense spending and interference into the affairs of other countries. The Democrats argue against further conflict. Since the end of World War II the US has been involved in roughly 63 military actions. If taken from a Republican perspective this indicates that business is based on creating a constant war economy, generating wealth and providing employment for those that need it under a war footing. Some sides of the legislative structure believe defense has better return for dollar invested while the other believes defense cost the country. The US has unconsciously assumed the role as the world's policeman, hence the large budget. It is time to share the burden.

Security goes beyond the role of policeman. Security necessitates that countries form an alliance and act for the interests of all in the alliance. National security must transform to international security by way of collective security for all countries in the alliance. Non-lethal conflict resolution has to be at the center of collective security. Non-lethal conflict resolution uses all available non-lethal technologies and weapons currently available to overthrow overly controlling countries. Using non-lethal technologies and tactics allows the majority of facilities, personnel, and secrets to be recovered from repressive rulers and provides the alliance forces a glimpse into the daily affairs and plans of repression—an intelligence bonanza.

Controlling countries tend to be unilateral and lethal. They organize a war hierarchy and a commitment to defense based on national security and unilateral interests. Their obsession fertilizes a nationalistic mentality and an overwhelming need for defense. Prompting fear and an arms race for other regional members. This strategy stimulates division and suspicion throughout the region.

An alliance of countries that practice non-lethal conflict resolution can offset the unilateral ambitions of a regional country. During the Cold War years, countries evolved based on progress of weapons. The evolution of weaponry such as catapults, swords, bows and arrows, armor and cross bows preceded the muskets, rifles, and cannons. With the introduction of black powder and petroleum production, a slow evolution toward mechanization got underway. This started the production of war materials and eventual addition of lethal weapons production as elements of the Gross National Product, the beginning of an influential arms industry. This resulted in the emergence of production line manufacturing and new approaches to management, job availability, and money flows. This birthed a new paradigm to transform the agrarian society to manufacturing. The research and production of non-lethal weapons and technologies introduces a new paradigm for this generation. It establishes a new foundation for: manufacturing, management, defense, international security, job growth, money-flows, and others. As a new paradigm it presents new technological, social, business, and personal interactions that take humanity to the next level of evolution.

The next paradigm partitions the world into regions of countries, free and repressive, with the ambitions of converting repressive countries to freedom. Initially, each region will be a market for free countries only. The regional markets will influence country participation and local job growth. While this approach appears to limit the market it actually creates more qualified customers in each region due to economic equalization and the ideological spread of freedom. The new paradigm provides quality products through cutting edge manufacturing and modern services. It restarts manufacturing specifically to produce non-lethal implements and quality regional goods. Enticing local entrepreneurs to build on their previously gained knowledge from making current lethal weapons and adopt a new defense position that will not weaken national security, but set new priorities for international and collective security.

Non-lethality is the evolution of conflict resolution from lethal abilities to non-lethal abilities. It creates a mental distinction of good guys (free countries and free militias) not killing and bad boys (the forces of control) killing. Within the transition of lethal to non-lethal global stability increases because paranoia and ill feelings diminishes, ultimately a community is formed. Thus the drive for non-lethal technologies will spark a spike in research and development as countries of the Free World attempt to develop and apply various technologies for operational use. People's exploration of non-lethal technologies for national and international security contributes to tackling the next of humanity's challenges—the environment by increasing technical knowledge about biological systems.

Non-lethality provides a new approach to defense and at its core—it takes into account human rights. Adherence to human rights removes hardships from people's lives and developing an environment for customizable behavior in a global middle class.

Philosophically this approach challenges the oppression and control of anyone. Freedom and human rights are linked. Organizations can monitor these and provide valuable insight into levels of control and freedom in each country. Since every Non-Governmental Organizations (NGO) produces their own annual report about human rights, combined with other international observations, gives analysts a relatively accurate assessment of people's freedom. Human rights organizations and the many free intelligence agencies provide information that can form a complete portrait of a country. As a catalyst this assessment can stimulate a global middle class gap by increasing the potential size of the middle class. Political scientists have categorized country types ad infinitum, the question is establishing the criteria to determine their degree of freedom or control.

Countries voluntarily join the free countries and the Free World if they adhere to strict a set of mandates. Compliance to these mandates is beneficial. The benefits come in the form of joint international security fortified by transitional membership into the ranks of modern, developed countries. Membership demands participants vow to adhere to a strict "no kill" policy. Part of a "no kill" policy is using all available non-lethal technologies such as examples of direct energy (the Active Denial or CHAMPS systems. Microwave technology for crowd control and electromagnetic pulse for knocking out electrical and electronic systems), kinetic (beanbag guns that replace bullets to knock targets down and do not break any skin), entrapments (net guns that can envelop a person or a vehicle), odorants (Stink bombs for dissuading people from a person or place), or calmatives (Different types of gas that demand clarification under the Geneva Convention). These technologies require advanced technical expertise so people will need to obtain high quality non-lethal knowledge. Non-lethality does not mean non-violence; it means the use of force short of killing. In terms of Mixed Martial Arts it means submitting an opponent or bringing them under control.

Killing is wrong. Kill and you have just lost the war. If foreign commanders understand that the ultimate objective of a military is not to enlist expendable people or causalities, they will think favorably about voluntarily joining such an non-lethal operation. A military committed to non-lethality can support the political ambitions of the international free community of countries, solidify international cohesion, and make contributions to freedom.

In order to defend the Free World and begin the transformation into a world-state, for matters of international security a global, non-lethal (way to distinguish the forces of freedom from the forces of control) military police force is needed. Instead of national funds being dedicated to individual country national security, they can be used to promote new non-lethal research and development to further international security. This strategy helps to reduce operational costs for countries and provides a means to establish a generous social safety net. The alliance and its research protect free countries from repression, international aggression and create a rapid multinational response force. Unlike deterrence theory this kind of security will not create an armed standoff. Optimism is achieved using tactics of collective security, understanding and non-lethality. Non-lethal weapons, technologies, and tactics distinguish the troops of the free bloc from those of their enemy. Repressive entities kill to get their way, the free bloc do not.

People that manufacture lethal armaments do not have to feel like they've reached the end of the employment road, they can transition to non-lethal weaponry and keep supporting defense. R&D can continue to pursue their lethal platforms, just take the design one module further. The opportunities are there with many frontline commanders asking for non-lethal technology to broaden their operational options. The most recent example was the proposed deployment of the Active Denial System in Iraq—concerned about it being perceived as a new torture device ended the proposal. Non-lethal technology has been used in many armed clashes. The Marines in Somalia used non-lethal technologies to assist in their withdrawal. In the Bosnian conflict, paint grenades were used to mark riot leaders for later capture. The use of rubber bullets has a mixed record. Tear gas is widely used in crowd control. Tasers and pepper spray have become standard equipment for many police forces. Within prison settings, crowd control has been strengthened by the use of stinger grenades—grenades that explode and propel hundreds of non-lethal pellets into a crowd. Some police departments use sticky foam, beanbag guns, retractable spike strips, anti-traction chemicals, and many more technologies to help them achieve a non-lethal resolution. In 2005, a cruise ship operating off Somali shores escaped from aggressive armed pirates by using sonic-directed energy (Long Range Acoustic Device) technology. This equipment has become standard technology for this region. There are many non-lethal technologies available; they are just waiting for tactical application.

Regional stability and employment opportunities can come from the transition from lethal to non-lethal systems. A transition such as this allows companies working on low-tech lethal systems to hire new personnel, distribute resources and technologies to non-lethal systems. In other words, further the evolution of weaponry.

In order for non-lethal technology to gain a foothold in defense, it requires a new method of collective security. The current defense theory of deterrence does not promote multilateral, voluntary, cooperative compliance. Unlike non-lethal technology, deterrence does not foster the groundwork for collective security. It perpetuates unilateral behavior and the continued spiral of defense costs. Using deterrence to force a country into compliance is just postponement until a country gets a bigger stick such as a nuclear weapon. Let's use North Korea as an example. Deterrence is not the answer. We need a new strategy.

A NEW
INFRASTRUCTURE

The new strategy could have an operational structure that promotes an integrated world-state, without black helicopters or prison camps. The new paradigm and strategy requires explanation. In this paradigm, development will no longer be step-by-step or by a competitive race, members that choose the side of freedom will become instant equal, economic superpowers. After World War II, Germany and Japan were given advances to the front of the development line. Today, they are doing well, economically, even though Japan maintains its xenophobic culture.

Persuading a controlling country to adopt freedom, unwillingly, will be difficult, but if a country wants to voluntarily convert then it is a whole different story. The World Bank, the International Monetary Fund (IMF) and free country development banks can provide the resources for the loans that initiate domestic growth repressive countries to change and provide them loans to get started.

Since the World Bank is dedicated to indiscriminate long-term development for countries in the world, a new revised World Bank must dedicate itself to ideology and not those of economic values. Currently, standard business models use convoluted economic models in mixed ideological countries to determine if a country is a success or not. In economic societies, economically prosperous equals a successful country. This completely avoids the ideology of the country or its long-term ambitions. Focusing on economic models disregards responsibility and strengthens the national impulse for immediate returns. Immediate development is not achieved by just giving money away. Long-term and short-term objectives can be reached by following the strategies of free organizations. Money is not just handed-out to a country; it is loaned. As success goes with various local organizations, the loans are paid back.

The IMF is dedicated to short-term development and poverty control based on financial trends and disregards any long-term ambitions or goals of any of its members. The current IMF attempts to fit every country into a predetermined economic hole regardless of ideology. In the new paradigm, development is contingent on ideological stance not economic possibilities.

Economic activities and boosts are limited to regional and state-of-the-art manufacturing and modern services. The primary emphasis is to expand the market from unruly and ideologically mixed international markets to three ideologically bound regional markets. Regional markets will only be making and selling domestic manufactured products and services. These will be high quality offerings since they will be coming from economic superpowers. Each region should be self-contained and, in an emergency, able to interact with other free regional countries outside of their market.

Creating an environment to promote freedom has existed for a long time. Adopting the ideologies of freedom and control will require the establishing of a new political infrastructure. The misconception is that peace must happen first before a country obtains freedom. Hence peace accords, peacekeepers, cease-fires, etc. that perpetuate armed standoffs and nonchalant behavior.

Not only does this approach for freedom change the political landscape, it mandates a set style for business. The ideologies of freedom and control create two polarized entities that are isolated from each other. The two entities of freedom and control do not trade with each other—isolation is paramount. Because freedom creates similar countries, economic rules are the same and cash flows within they can be accurately portrayed—unlike North Korea where knowledge about the flow of money is limited.

Unlike previous philosophies, a freedom philosophy does not force an economic model on society or coerce a society to adhere to it. It is not a push strategy, but a voluntary pull strategy. An incentive is to willingly adopt this philosophy and to pull others into it.

A new infrastructure needs to be uncontrolled and founded on distinct ideologies of freedom and control. It allows natural forces to function in a country. It takes a holistic view of the situation without assuming a self-defining economic model that isolates a country from all other countries in the world. This new approach undertakes a microscopic economic analysis on a country, such as market forces or business cycles in a regional sense and in the context of overall freedom. Macroscopic economic analysis determines if a country is participatory or controlling. In the new infrastructure, ideology will not be limited to one country, but it will review a group of countries that share the same philosophy. The new philosophy accepts the ideological duality of existence and identifies the two polar entities.

The element missing in most country assessments is the degree of human rights concurrence. Figure 1 details the varying degrees of freedom and repression. Countries can be categorized by their degree of freedom, placing them into categories from best to worst.

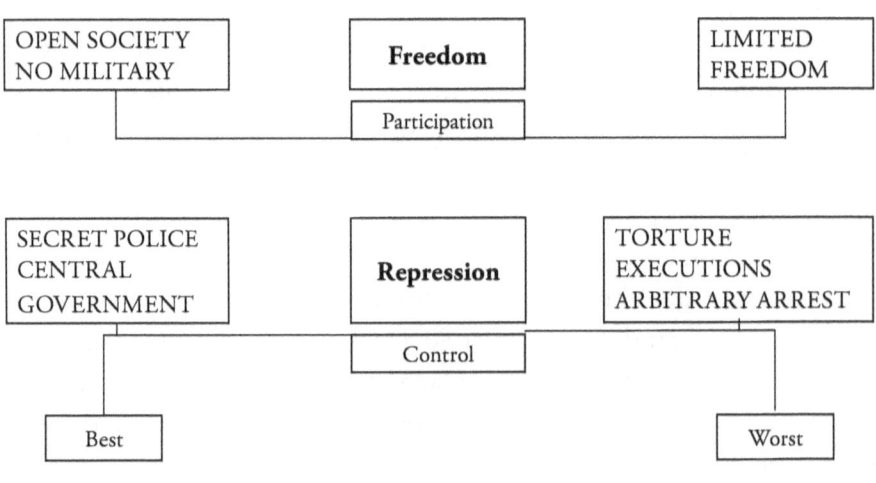

Figure 1.

Countries with the worst degrees of control can be identified for imminent action by of a new United Nations and the Free World using an ideological international military police force. An international military police force is different from INTERPOL, it is based on universal laws of freedom and compliance, laws that supersede national laws, and it is able to enforce international decrees. It is approved and supported by every free country. This organization actively addresses every incidence of control. It maintains a force of military policemen from every free country. Any action it takes has the unanimous approval of every free country and the United Nations made of countries that believe in freedom.

A free UN organization will be the world's only military superpower, but only equipped for non-lethal conflict. It is made up of voluntary personnel from each free country. As a way to separate the organization from any Cold War baggage, (a country must adhere to agreed-upon international standards of behavior) and since it has very strict rules for membership with no repressive baggage, countries like Russia and the People's Republic of China will be able to join if they become free as judged by the free international community. Economics will not be used to influence their eligibility. No Cold War baggage, there would not be any ideological debate between communism and capitalism. Once ideological issues are settled they can become members of the organization—take action and use both communist and capitalist forward-operating sites and regional defense groups to assist in its mission of non-lethal intervention. Using the diagram above, the organization would determine the degree of repression in targeted countries and assign an intervention priority to it.

The purpose of assigning an intervention priority identifies the seriousness of potential offenders of repression and control. The severest offenders are given a high priority, and after a review by the entire Free World and the free United Nations, political and non-military moves are made to stimulate a change before action is taken against them. Once a unanimous decision to repel a country's internal control is made, the organization would intervene. Since intervention is initiated with non-lethal technologies, women could be part of the front-line of troops.

Two tactics are characteristic of this organization—overwhelming numbers and non-lethality.

An example of this would be with Burma or Myanmar, as the repressive rulers wish to call it. Since it is as a country that is highly repressive, it would be identified for intervention. Previous regional military bases around Burma are activated as forward-operating sites. The United Nations and the Free World begin actions to isolate it, a political and material blockade begins. Free countries in the region deploy personnel to the forward-operating sites. The free countries provide the manpower and regional expertise, and the UN provides the latest non-lethal technology. All of this is done publicly because the primary object here is psychological; to let Burmese troops know what is in store for them. The underlying message is that they will be defeated and captured. No one dies at the Free World's hands. A lot of troops will be positioned at their borders. If a country registers on the repression spectrum, it will be given steps to reverse the intervention priority. Countries can voluntarily adopt a new degree of ideological standing and map out a path for improvement. The criteria for this evolution can be found at the end of this manual.

Nuclear weapons and many conventional arms intimidate and would not be needed in a world based on freedom. Nuclear weapons do not foster multilateral cooperation and collective security they only foster suspicion and reaction.

Possessing a bigger stick to deter an opponent only injects instability into a region. Look at what this has done for Iran and North Korea. Their pursuit of nuclear weapons, the big stick, has created turmoil in their respective regions. It has put them under an international spotlight and stuck them with the name of pariah. Proliferation of lethal weapons and a philosophy of control mark them as new clients for arms merchants and a concern for international peace. Continuing defense based on the idea of dissuading the enemy perpetuates the constant search for a bigger stick.

Bigger or the more effectiveness of a weapon only ensures a bigger counter reaction. Power of intimidation is short lived as a teeter-top game unfolds and balance is reestablished. Intimidation is not measured in the number or types of weapons, but balance. Searching for balance is not really about balance it is about strategic advantage. Proliferation melds well with a unilateral strategy of react and counter. Many entities feel power comes from the amount of destruction and death they can cause; the more the merrier. A goal for them becomes—nuclear weapons. North Korea and Iran share this drive. Like most countries they believe the mentality that accompanies deterrence—once they cross the nuclear threshold, all weapons acquisition contests are over. Acquiring nuclear weapons is not nirvana. It just means a new threshold of problems now applies. Destruction with conventional arms does not mean disregard the nuclear barrier, but proliferation happens with conventional or non-conventional weapons. Only non-lethal conflict resolution can leash proliferation. In the meanwhile, proliferation will continue.

Nuclear weapons are one of many weapons that can cause extensive death and destruction. Lethal evolution of weapons went from deadly to very deadly and destructive to precision strike weapons, like drone attacks. Evolution of weapons has opened the doors to non-lethal weapons. Value is assigned to weapons that cause the most deaths. Evolution of weapons in the 21st Century will value the ability to not kill. Society and humanity will view killing as a sign of ignorant thinking and frown on it. Having nuclear weapons is a sign of society being stuck in evolution and not being a modern state.

Possessing advanced lethal weapons and systems in every region of the world increases the possibility of proliferation and regional arms competition in a search for balance. A UN representative said that in the past 15 years, 7 million weapons have been brought into Central Africa alone. According to 2014 statistics there are more than 875 million arms in circulation worldwide. Ultimately, the presence of various weapons and systems in opposition militaries increases the vulnerability of some countries and leads to regional instability. For instance, putting the Patriot anti-missile system in Poland has stimulated reactive regional concern by the Russians.

Proliferation is used to maintain balance through weapons; it also reinforces the belief of kill or be killed. A misconception about war is that it is uncontrollable. To achieve a controllable state in conflict or war requires assuming that war is a conflict, one of many. War or conflict is defined as use of a strategy to make macro decisions for military units acting in conjunction to a geographically dispersed target. Controllability comes when any conflict is kept at the tactical level or surgically managed at the micro level. Controlling conflict is a vehicle to attain strategic advantage and for introducing new weapons systems.

Any new lethal weapons system increases the volatility of the region by throwing balance out the window. An opponent in turn introduces a counter system to restore its sense of strategic advantage or balance. This will prompt the other side to respond in kind. So begins the arms spiral. India and Pakistan demonstrated this. When the Indians exploded a nuclear bomb and shortly thereafter Pakistan exploded its nuclear weapon to return to a sense of balance and the spiral continues to this day. An Indian Congressional leader Mani Shankar Aiyar said, "We had a strong conventional military advantage over Pakistan....the minute we became a nuclear weapon power....it took Pakistan three weeks to become a nuclear weapons power themselves."

Under deterrence, proliferation is inevitable because people perceive that power is based on weapons. Deterrence implies that power comes from the number of weapons a country has or its capability to maintain strategic advantage with weapons. Under deterrence each country becomes a marketplace for additional weaponry and is drawn into proliferation. Under previous perceptions of balance, there is a constant growth in the number of available weapons and the ability to upgrade systems is a constant possibility; which leads to a growing defense budget. More money for defense means less for society.

Concern for proliferation should not be limited to nuclear, biological, or chemical weapons (NBC). The events of 911 in New York, Washington, and Pennsylvania, 411 bombings in Madrid, the 77 London bombings, the Bali bombing, the attack on the US embassies, the USS Cole, and so on, clearly indicate that NBC weapons are not the only avenue for high body counts. Conventional weapons should not be overlooked. It is foolish to think that nuclear, biologic, or chemical weapons are the only weapons that can yield high body counts. Proliferation should be considered for all weapons that kill. Efficiency and effectiveness is usually determined by body count and maintains the military and war as destructive uncontrollable entities.

Using a non-lethal strategy and prohibitive trade policies, the Free World arms manufacturers will not be able supply a constant trickle of lethal weapons and systems to angry countries. Under a non-lethal strategy, the only weapons that will be available are a limited supply of non-lethal weapons. Currently in the competition for lethal arms sales the US leads the pact—it is: 1) USA, 2) Russia, 3) Germany (FRG), 4) France, 5) UK, 6) Spain, 7) the PRC, 8) Israel, 9) Netherlands, and 10) Italy. A non-lethal strategy would stop this competition and aid in reducing proliferation, improving relations and the world's financial situation.

National security concerns emphasize unilateralism and nationalism. A national security perspective takes attention away from unity and collective security. A holistic global policy that considers the international community must exceed national security interests and focus on international security. Patriotism is not a nation-state issue; it should be viewed worldwide. A country is not defined by economic ability, but ideals that guide its ideology. Patriotism has not been reached because one country is comfortable. Until everyone is comfortable; the job is not done. Human rights records are a key determinant in ideological stance and a step towards comfort.

Although the US has the largest defense budget of any country and a person would be correct in saying its budget is more than the next 5 countries. It swallows the entire cost of being the world's global military police force. Basically it has adopted the role of reluctant go-to guy.

REGIONALIZATION

Every region should have one quality, dedicated, independent self-sustaining market for free countries. A new infrastructure isolates free countries from repressive countries, and create unique, distributed but sustaining markets. Each market expands regional production for manufacturing and services. The world can be divided into three main regions. One region is North America, Central and Latin Americas, and the Caribbean countries. Another region is Europe and the African countries. The final region is Asian countries, Australia, and Pacific Ocean countries. It all depends on partitioning.

Regionalization creates achievable regions that improve the quality of life and stimulate funds for the region. Each region's strength challenges external threats, provides an avenue for the free marketing of quality services and products, and is self-sufficient. Regionalization is non-coercive. It is a business decision that is voluntary. Countries that pursue regionalization put their faith in market forces and people. Regionalization uses a pull tactic that encourages voluntary participation. It focuses on a country's unique service or product instead of trying to provide both manufacturing and services. The key emphasis of regionalization is cooperation not competition. Comparative advantage—focusing on single, unique, local, quality, and equal products or services—these are products or services that fulfill regional demand and are ready for international demand.

A free country does not establish an equal global economy. Instead, they create environments for free regional countries to sell quality goods to countries that cannot produce these products. The objective of regionalization is to create local markets to meet local employment and business needs with quality. It provides the means for equal products and services to compliment each other. Markets provide opportunities where regional free countries establish economic relations and form defense alliances.

Regionalization creates markets with similar ideological beliefs. It integrates the many different regional segments of individual societies into a monolith of unity. This new ideal or new facet of the freedom ideology incorporates trade and freedom through regionalization. Regionalization binds all countries to freedom. Foremost, each country's citizens are unrestrained, free, and share complete voluntary participation in the political affairs of their country. Regionalization determines membership to see if a country belongs in the international community. It forces countries to get off the indecision fence, non-aligned or neutral, take an ideological stance, and assume responsibility for the affairs of their countries, their people and their managers.

All participants in these markets exploit freethinking and entrepreneurship with their products or services. The only limit for these markets is that they do not trade with any country practicing control or repression. Trade relies on voluntary participation, demand and the acceptance of other free countries in the region. The adoption of freedom and approval of other free countries is a green flag for participation. It gives people trading access to a true global market.

Freedom allows people to pursue entrepreneurial efforts and provide job creation that does not perpetuate a war economy. The availability of local, regional employment prevents people seeking jobs in far-off countries. Reducing immigration and creating jobs increases the stability of the region. Jobs are not just about becoming economic slaves to an employer, it addresses the people that accomplish tasks around the home. Such as cleaning duties, watching the children, landscaping, herd management, etc. This is where the importance of multigenerational families coming together encourages more of a nuclear family. It allots employment into two categories: money-winners and home sustainers.

An awareness of local customs and needs will effectively target products and services for local businesses. Regional cultures and customs fulfill local user needs and do not create artificial desires for an item to lower market expenses. In free regional markets geographic proximity makes replacement parts and maintenance easier to obtain. All communication and transportation costs are regional. The consumer is close to manufacturers and consumer services. These regional markets contribute to the success of a new infrastructure and a new future.

THE ENVIRONMENT

The environment cannot be ignored. Ignoring it and hoping it will heal itself is unrealistic, as some Republicans want to do. Embarking on policies that impose limits on society will not work either, as some Democrats want to do. Being a denier or an alarmist is not the healthy way or productive way of solving the problem.

A solution is to stop establishing large energy, large supply, and large storage operations that are driven by an imaginary global market. Develop new smaller systems that are portable and efficient for regional use. Make energy units small so that they can be put in a backpack and people can take them as they pioneer.

One of the main culprits attacking the environment is global warming. It does not matter who or what caused global warming. It is happening. The UN Climate Change Secretariat indicates that is occurring. In the course of research, groups from the Australian National University and the British Antarctica Survey have made conclusions that climate change is at its worse in over 1,000 years. Climate researchers have seen glaciers that are melting and receding, polar ice caps melting, endangered polar bears, extreme weather, and ozone depletion, among others. It is unlikely that pointing fingers is going to change anything. Chances are nothing can be done to permanently keep it from happening; however, we might be able to have an impact on its severity. Although predictions from the 2011 Intergovernmental Panel on Climate Change reported drastic change in the weather and how people affect it, the 2012 report is more factual given how the 2011 report is speculative. In 2014 a review of the IPCC reports summarized them as the initial report pointed out the existence of climate change or global warming, the 2012 report indicated the consequences of climate change, the 2014 report stipulates some of the options to slow it down, and the 2016 report will outline the impacts of these options.

People structure laws to ensure permanence in their life. People like permanence and blame others when they lose it. The enemy of permanence is change. There is no one to blame for change. Change is natural and the only thing left to do is accept it. The world is changing. People cannot go against nature. To do so is a fool's folly. If this is difficult to comprehend, just think about the unsinkable Titanic. Nothing man-made can win in a fight with nature.

Global warming shows that even though attempts have been made to keep nature from changing, it continues to change—the Green Movement in India and the beginnings before the Dust Bowl in the US. People tried to unsuccessfully mold and control the world with man-made visions of resource development. Change happens every day. People think they are in complete control, but nature lets them know differently. Attempts have been made to deal with nature in a number of ways to control it and nature lashed back ten fold with the Indian Ocean tsunami, the southern USA's Hurricanes Katrina and Rita, Hurricane Sandy, Mount Montserrat's eruption, the People's Republic of China's earthquake, the Central Asian earthquake, or Japan's Kobe earthquake. As we add more noise pollution in the oceans and seas what will be the kickback—more tsunamis, more beaching, a bigger island of plastic and trash in sea, the extinction of all fish before they are fished out?

The challenge for the environment is to establish regional superiority and freedom for all people, creating conditions to protect large groups of humanity and eventually the environment by customizing refined modern technology. Regions and new technologies can be strengthened. The development of new technologies comes from increased attention and social structures allowing people unrestricted travel to any place they desire and still enjoy modernity. Modernity is something that should be the shared from region to region.

Travel and pioneering are synonymous. Travel implies a visit and pioneering implies you move there. Pioneering should be enticing and innovative, but at the same time environmentally friendly. Pioneering suggests physical freedom. Pioneering is not covered wagons and rustic living; it is adventure. It is using modern tools to explore and adapt. As more technology becomes portable, people will be flexible and meet their energy needs while adapting to the environment. Pioneers will recruit many members of their dispersed families into their efforts. Multi-generational families will join together and use new technologies to explore distant free homelands. Within these families subsistence jobs provide a home where monetary job employees can have a base to operate from.

Current political delineations, such as borders, have major impacts on people. Borders divide land and are create barriers for political power brokers and regions. Many boundaries cut through tribes and cultures. Each country's culture forced to development in accord with the environment that enveloped it. Each culture adapted to geographical location and local beliefs. New customs added to the culture as it adapted to a new location. It was a continuous cycle of adaptation and change.

Migration also influenced global warming. Although migrations are viewed as steps in human growth, populated areas result in deforestation, water shortages, overpopulation concerns, and pollution. Things like toxic chemicals, coruption of the water tables, overflowing landfills, light pollution, etc., damage the environment. Cities provide a valuable service to humanity, but they are concentration points for pollution that assault the environment. Wherever there is a collection of people, there is a concentration of pollution.

Pollution management or environmentalism presents an opportunity to expand on technologies produced in the fight against repression. The transition from a successful war on repression to a war on pollution provides evolutionary industry research and production goals for future employment. A defining event will mark the beginning of the environment conflict. At this point plans and resource allocation can be made. Transitioning to a new technological cycle adds stability to the financial crisis and uses resources and personnel that were critical assets and expertise in the struggle against repression. To clean up the environment, people must first deal with repression.

Most of the global community is arrogant because of religious beliefs and neglect the world's environment. The environment is a secondary concern. Defense theories of deterrence and its applications have allowed the Free World to create a state of constant political fear with images and thoughts of terrorists, subversives, or sleeper cells. Although the environment is a critical threat to people's welfare, it pales in comparison to the threat of coercive power through repression and death. Repression and its followers are the most pressing threat before tackling the environment. Repressive rulers have shown how one individual can motivate others to undermine environmental concerns. Saddam Hussein did this after the invasion of Kuwait by ordering the ignition of all the Kuwait's oil wells to cover the Iraqi Army's retreat in 1991, and pouring oil into the gulf (January 1991) during Desert Storm. Mao Zedong also showed his disregard for environmental concerns when he ordered the construction of smelters in the back yards of all homes (1958-1960) in the People's Republic of China during the Cultural Revolution. One person can have a major impact on the environment if repression is not confronted.

People have shown that modern demands for energy can be met if repression is held in check. Regionally specific methods can be used to generate the power. Modern tools demand a lot of power that can be provided with various technologies. Combining solar energy with wind power can provide enough power to meet the demands of modern tools. The average modern house uses about 11,496 kWh per year. These power demands for non-grid approaches. Future technologies such as residential fuel cells will be able to contribute to power requirements, as will geothermal, solar, wind, or wave.

A key environmental threat is the belief that things must get bigger in order to be successful. This counters the philosophy behind miniaturization. Miniaturization is the issue of quality versus size. Conventional thinking states that business operations must get larger; we must produce more; our vehicles and living space must get bigger;

and our markets must increase in size. "Bigger is better" has been drummed into business people's psyche. Environmental vulnerability has increased because of this. Large oil operations transporting on large ships across the ocean, population migration into cities, and irrigation are just a few examples of the threat. Since the number of food producers is declining, acquisition increases and farms get bigger as they are transformed into corporate farms and in its mutant form—Agribusiness. These corporate farms must meet production quotas, so they introduce genetically modified seed to guarantee output.

By pulling further away from smaller practices and world problems, putting all resources toward large productions the possibility of chaos rises. Vulnerabilities have made their presence known with poor air quality, brown outs and black outs, water shortages, and oil slicks. Each of these vulnerabilities has a different impact on our world. Hence, the Exxon Valdez oil spill or the rolling power outages, or the Midwest power outage in August 2003. Large systems can have great impact when things go wrong. Presently, successful wind and solar farms are being created, but they are also large, which bring on these vulnerabilities of small and big.

To become environmentally proficient, we have to modify the international community by encouraging the spread of freedom and ensure technological pioneering. This requires a complete revision of the way we live. In order to confront the challenge of global warming and other forms of environmental damage, we must begin thinking small customizable technologies and finding ways to adapt. Ideally, we seek out reliable energy systems such as individual photovoltaic systems on rooftops, individual windmills, residential fuel cells, geothermal, wave energy, environmentally friendly building materials, and other technological products that have yet to be produced.

Any recognition of global warming or acknowledgment of environmental issues does not mean giving up. It means taking an active role in the situation. We redefine our concept of sovereignty, energy and power. Successes come from changing the structure of nation-states and begin looking at the entire world holistically, such as a world-state. We recognize our problems on a global scale. We do not have to give up our technological advances, but modify them so that they no longer threaten the environment. The regional impacts of global warming depend on our ability to adapt to a non-permanent world. Even if global warming is natural progression, adaption is not.

Expanding regionalization and freedom raises wages and benefits, thereby lessening losses to immigration and drawing families into one geographic location. In the future, families can be multi-generational and work together as a money-producing survival group, both subsistence and monetary workers. The emphasis on smaller technologies and collective security allows us to explore, settle, and still be modern families. This provides immigrants and family members the incentive to return home.

We, in every free country, must provide a TEMPORARY haven for other regional people as they seek to escape repression and deplete manpower from repressive countries. The most important thing we can do is not to label them as legal or illegal immigrants, but as escapees with a desire for a free homeland. The world is a free world, a complete united holistic entity—not a collection of individual entities with different perspectives.

In conclusion, there is reason to be optimistic about the future. It can be better for everyone and the groundwork exists to make things better generation by generation. The choice is simply whether we choose to be free or repressed.

CRITERIA FOR ASSESSMENT

This section provides criteria needed to exam each country and to determine ideological foundation whether it is free or repressed. Assessing countries of the world is just an issue of control and laxity. Some countries have respect for their citizens and the pursuit of well-being.

The scales of 10 to 1 are categories of
worst (more control) to best (to least control).

Scales of Repression

Repression 10

- **Non-communist dictator or monarchy**—control of government centered in strongman's grip. Considers self above the law and people are willing to reinforce this belief.
- **Result of a coup or inheritance**—control of government by force or continuation of the philosophy.
- **No elections**—control of electoral process.
- **Trampled all opposition**—removed all domestic political challenges.
- **Military emphasis**—power base.
- **No environmental concerns**—only concerned with economics and survival.

- **Refugee problem**—reaction to internal politics and their view of the future.
- **Secret police**—indicates the trust government has in its citizens.
- **No civil rights for public**—laws made by the dictator to support the regime.
- **Strong police and military**—power-base for foreign and domestic influences.
- **Intense people control**—to reinforce the dictates of the regime.
- **Serious human rights violations**—executions, torture, and imprisonment.

Repression 9

- **Communist dictator**—system to support communist ideology.
- **Result of a coup**—non-elected takeover of government.
- **No elections**—control of electoral process.
- **Trampled all opposition**—removed all domestic political challenges.
- **Military emphasis**—power base.
- **No environmental concerns**—only concerned with economics and survival.
- **Refugee problem**—citizen reaction to internal politics and their view of the future.
- **Secret police**—indicates the trust government has in its citizens.
- **No civil rights for public**—laws made by the dictator to support the regime.
- **Strong police and military**—power-base for foreign and domestic influences.
- **Intense people control**—to reinforce the dictates of the regime.•••
- **Serious human rights violations**—executions, torture, and imprisonment.

Repression 8

- **Non-communist dictator or absolute monarchy**—ruler defined by single person.
- **Result of coup or inheritance laws**—interpreted by custom or outside group.
- **No elections**—control of electoral process.
- **No environmental concerns**—only concerned with economics and survival.
- **Secret police**—indicates the trust government has in its citizens.
- **No civil rights for public**—laws made by the dictator to support the regime.
- **Strong police and military**—power-base for foreign and domestic influences.
- **Intense people control**—to reinforce the dictates of the regime.
- **Serious human rights violations**—executions, torture, and imprisonment.

Repression 7

- **Communist dictator or strong leader**—head of government.
- **Controlled election**—government influenced elections.
- **One party**—no opposition.
- **Secret police**—domestic power-base.
- **Non-secret election**—government monitored.
- **Military emphasis**—alliance with government.
- **Refugee problem**—citizen reaction to internal politics and their view of the future.
- **No environmental concerns**—only concerned with economics and survival.
- **People control**—society seeks to maintain control over at least one group of society.
- **Strong police and military**—power-base for foreign and domestic influences.

- **Serious human rights violations**—executions, torture, and imprisonment.

Repression 6

- **Figure head**—spokesman for policy.
- **Result of successor or inheritance**—desire to have continuity in government.
- **People outside govt. give direction**—national focus of elections.
- **Multi-party election**—opposition parties.
- **Unrealistic opposition**—government controlled.
- **Secret police**—indicates the trust government has in its citizens.
- **Non-secret election**—government monitored.
- **No environmental concerns**—only concerned with economics and survival.
- **Military emphasis**—alliance with government.
- **Refugee problem**—citizen reaction to internal politics and their view of the future.
- **People control**—society seeks to maintain control over at least one group of society.
- **Strong police and military**—power-base for foreign and domestic influences.
- **Serious human rights violations**—executions, torture, and imprisonment.

Repression 5

- **Communist figure head**—Politburo in charge of government.
- **Centrally planned**—5 or 7-year production plans.
- **Unrealistic opposition**—government controlled.
- **Secret police**—indicates the trust government has in its citizens.
- **Non-secret election**—government monitored.
- **No environmental concerns**—only concerned with economics and survival.

- **Military emphasis**—alliance with government.
- **Refugee problem**—citizen reaction to internal politics and their view of the future.
- **People control**—society seeks to maintain control over at least one group of society.
- **Strong police and military**—power-base for foreign and domestic influences.
- **Human rights violations**—arrests and imprisonment.

Repression 4

- **No environmental concerns**—only concerned with economics and survival.
- **Non-secret election**—government monitored.
- **Questionable civil rights**—government appears to randomly set laws.
- **Secret police**—indicates the trust government has in its citizens.
- **Shady elections**—validity questionable.
- **Multi-party election**—opposition parties.
- **Military emphasis**—alliance with government.
- **Refugee problem**—citizen reaction to internal politics and their view of the future.
- **People control**—society seeks to maintain control over at least one group of society.
- **Strong police and military**—power-base for foreign and domestic influences.
- **Human rights violations**—arrests and imprisonment.

Repression 3

- **Socialist or nationalistic government involvement** in private sector.
- **Multi-party election**—opposition parties.
- **No environmental concerns**—only concerned with economics and survival.
- **Non-secret election**—government monitored.
- **Questionable civil rights**—government appears to randomly set laws.
- **Shady elections**—validity questionable.
- **People control**—society seeks to maintain control over at least one group of society.
- **Strong police and military**—power-base for foreign and domestic influences.
- **Human rights violations**—arrests and imprisonment.

Repression 2

- **People control**—society seeks to maintain control over at least one group of society.
- **Multi-party election**—opposition parties.
- **Questionable civil rights**—government appears to randomly set laws.
- **Shady elections**—validity questionable.
- **No environmental concerns**—only concerned with economics and survival.
- **Non-secret election**—government monitored.
- **Strong police**—domestic control rather intense.
- **Accusations of human rights violations**—non-serious charges for violations from human rights groups.

Repression 1

- **Socialist or nationalistic government involvement**—in private sector.
- **People control**—society seeks to maintain control over at least one group of society.
- **Multi-party election**—opposition parties.
- **Secret elections**—no monitoring.
- **Strong police**—domestic control rather intense.
- **Accusations of human rights violations**—non-serious charges for violations from human rights groups.

Scales of freedom

(worst {least permissive}
to best) {most permissive}

Freedom 10

- **Freedom rights**— Generally respects the freedom rights of its citizens.
- **Encourages economical freedom**—primary policy emphasis deals with improving the economy.
- **Thriving business**—entrepreneurial attitudes towards contributing to the economy.
- **Military oriented**—wavers in belief that humans are good.
- **Permissive society**—encourages entrepreneurialism.
- **Multi-party elections**—participation in political process.
- **Secret voting**—concerns for freedom of political direction.

Freedom 9

- **Freedom rights**— Generally respects the freedom rights of its citizens.
- **Encourages economical freedom**—primary policy emphasis deals with improving the economy.
- **Encourages personal freedom**—primary policy emphasis deals with measures to ward off imprisonment.
- **Thriving business**—entrepreneurial attitudes towards contributing to the economy.
- **Military oriented**—wavers in belief that humans are good.
- **Permissive society**—encourages entrepreneurialism.
- **Multi-party election**—opposition parties.
- **Secret voting**—no monitoring.

Freedom 8

- **Freedom rights**— Generally respects the freedom rights of its citizens.
- **Encourages spiritual freedom**—government does not dictate the path of spiritual growth.
- **Encourages economical freedom**—primary policy emphasis deals with improving the economy.
- **Encourages personal freedom**—primary policy emphasis deals with measures to ward off imprisonment.
- **Thriving business**—entrepreneurial attitudes towards contributing to the economy.
- **Military oriented**—wavers in belief that humans are good.
- **Permissive society**—encourages entrepreneurialism.
- **Multi-party elections**—participation in political process.
- **Secret voting**—concerns for freedom of political direction.

Freedom 7

- **Freedom rights**— Generally respects the freedom rights of its citizens.
- **Encourages intellectual freedom**—primary policy emphasis deals with expanding cognitive abilities.
- **Encourages spiritual freedom**—government does not dictate the path of spiritual growth.
- **Encourages economical freedom**—primary policy emphasis deals with improving the economy.
- **Encourages personal freedom**—primary policy emphasis deals with measures to ward off imprisonment.
- **Thriving business**—entrepreneurial attitudes towards contributing to the economy.
- **Permissive society**—encourages entrepreneurialism.
- **Multi-party elections**—participation in political process.
- **Secret voting**—concerns for freedom of political direction.

Freedom 6

- **Freedom rights**— Generally respects the freedom rights of its citizens.
- **Permits intellectual freedom**—policy directed to support intellectual growth.
- **Permits spiritual freedom**—no governmental guidance on the path of spiritual growth.
- **Permits economical freedom**—with improving the economy.
- **Permits personal freedom**—rules to ward off imprisonment.
- **Thriving business**—entrepreneurial attitudes towards contributing to the economy.
- **Switch from a military orientation to civilian technology**—developed for civilian world not the military world.
- **Multi-party elections**—participation in political process.
- **Secret voting**—concerns for freedom of political direction.

Freedom 5

- **Freedom rights**— Generally respects the freedom rights of its citizens.
- **Constitutional monarchy**—although a monarchy in country government control rests in elected hands.
- **Permits intellectual freedom**—policy directed to support intellectual growth.
- **Permits spiritual freedom**—no governmental guidance on the path of spiritual growth.
- **Permits economical freedom**—with improving the economy.
- **Permits personal freedom**—rules to ward off imprisonment.
- **Thriving business**—entrepreneurial attitudes towards contributing to the economy.
- **Switch from a military orientation to civilian technology**—developed for civilian world not the military world.
- **Multi-party elections**—participation in political process.
- **Secret voting**—concerns for freedom of political direction.

- **Environmental considerations**—concern about the environment.

Freedom 4

- **Freedom rights**— Generally respects the freedom rights of its citizens.
- **Permits intellectual freedom**—policy directed to support intellectual growth.
- **Permits spiritual freedom**—no governmental guidance on the path of spiritual growth.
- **Permits economical freedom**—with improving the economy.
- **Permits personal freedom**—rules to ward off imprisonment.
- **Focus on challenges facing humanity**—contributing to the economy.
- **Business by market demand**—invisible hand drives market.
- **Environmental considerations**—concern about the environment.
- **Multi-party elections**—participation in political process.
- **Secret voting**—concerns for freedom of political direction.

Freedom 3

- **Freedom rights**— Generally respects the freedom rights of its citizens.
- **Permits intellectual freedom**—policy directed to support intellectual growth.
- **Permits spiritual freedom**—no governmental guidance on the path of spiritual growth.
- **Permits economical freedom**—with improving the economy.
- **Permits personal freedom**—rules to ward off imprisonment.
- **Focus on challenges facing humanity**—concerned about the future, welfare concerns.
- **Job growth**—economy on the move upward.

- **Regionalization**—economic demand determined by need and philosophical disposition.
- **Environmental considerations**—concern about the environment.
- **Multi-party elections**—participation in political process.
- **Secret voting**—concerns for freedom of political direction.

Freedom 2

- **Freedom rights**— Generally respects the freedom rights of its citizens.
- **Open society**—whether right or wrong, all aspects of society can be reviewed.
- **Permits intellectual freedom**—policy directed to support intellectual growth.
- **Permits spiritual freedom**—no governmental guidance on the path of spiritual growth.
- **Permits economical freedom**—with improving the economy.
- **Permits personal freedom**—rules to ward off imprisonment.
- **Focus on challenges facing humanity**—concerned about the future, welfare concerns.
- **Thriving business**—entrepreneurial attitudes towards contributing to the economy.
- **Regionalization**—economic demand determined by need and philosophical disposition.
- **Environmental considerations**—concern about the environment.
- **Humanity welfare considerations**—concerned about the welfare of others.
- **Multi-party elections**—participation in political process.
- **Secret voting**—concerns for freedom of political direction.

Freedom 1

- **Freedom rights**— Generally respects the freedom rights of its citizens.
- **Open society**—press and citizens have complete access to information.
- **Grants intellectual freedom**—policies and philosophy about mental growth.
- **Grants spiritual freedom**—policies and philosophy about spirituality.
- **Grants economical freedom**—policies and philosophy about growth and the economy.
- **Grants personal freedom**—policies and philosophy on imprisonment.
- **Focus on challenges facing humanity**—concern for political direction.
- **Full employment**—empirical measure of political/citizen unity and freedom.
- **Thriving business**—entrepreneurial attitudes towards contributing to the economy.
- **Regionalization**—economic demand determined by need and philosophical disposition.
- **Civilian oriented**—directed towards growth of citizen policing.
- **Environmental considerations**—concern about the environment.
- **Humanity welfare considerations**—society totally concerned about human welfare and works to reduce imprisonment.
- **Multi-party elections**—participation in political process.
- **Secret voting**—concerns for freedom of political direction and citizen participation in choosing direction.

TYPES OF NON-LETHAL TECHNOLOGY

10 ga. Stinger Shells: for shotguns, stuns at ranges over 9m.

12 ga. Stinger Shells: for shotguns, stuns at ranges over 9m.

Acoustic psycho-correction affects the mind of the target. Useful for crowd control and to enhance special operations forces.

Acoustic systems Can stun targets and induce nausea or diarrhea, acoustic weapons could be mounted on helicopters, humvees or armored personnel carriers, promising a wide array of delivery options for maximum effectiveness. Acoustic weapons resonate at certain frequencies to vibrate the internal organs of targeted personnel.

Anti-traction Lubes to make it impossible to steer.

Arasaka Dart Rifle M101 A big game type gun related to the Simpson hunting rifles.

Arasaka Restraint Caster A spreading and immobilizing polymer that can hit a target any place and immobilize it. A pistol that fires a capsule of reactive material which upon contact with the atmosphere, assumes a semi solid form and spreads into long tendrils of polymer.

Backseat air bag Restraint system. More for law enforcement to control violent arrested suspects.

Barrier foam system A soap suds like material that covers an area of about 200 feet long and about 20 feet wide and around three to four feet high. Basically for crowd control. Tear gas agent incorporated into it.

Bean-bag weapon A riot gun that fire tiny beanbags. Safer than rubber bullets which can be lethal at close range. Beanbags will knock a man down.

Biotech-Askari Motion Restraint Bomb A hand thrown bomb that release a web polymer material. Prevents rapid or violent movements.

Chemicals Eats through bridges and structures, polymers to clog jet intake valves, and turn gas into jelly. Aerosol-delivered liquids turn metal brittle.

Chem Grenade Explodes filling air with atomized spray of drugs of choice. Does not work against sealed targets.

Concealed arms detection system A means of assessing a target to see if they have concealed weapons. Does not require that a target walk through a metal detector.

Concussion Grenade Upon detonation, all in a 4m radius will be stunned.

Constitution Arms Deluge Crowd Control Weapon A large machine cannon which fires polymer. A crowd control weapon that can manage a riot in a matter of minutes. Uses Sleep drugs.

Directed energy systems Emits a high energy electromagnetic pulses into the chassis and engine of modern computer controlled vehicles. These pulses either cause the engine control system to malfunction, or cause damage that makes the system inoperable. Does not affect safety systems such as braking and steering, the targeted vehicle's engine will die and cannot be turned over again.

Dye hand grenades: Crowd control and identify their leaders with dye. The size of little water balloons filled with dye that can mark the leaders or agitators or crowds so that they can be located later on by law enforcement authorities. Can be made to knock people down at a range of 15 to 30 yards.

Dynatech Industries Hand Taser A hand taser, that must touch the skin.

Electromagnetics gun Causes targets to go into an epileptic fit.

Electromagnetic pulse Non-nuclear pulse zaps radios, computers and lighting circuits or any of the target's electronic systems. Can be used against human targets can heat a target like a microwave oven, ranging from discomfort, or fever depending on the distance.

Enertex Power Squirt Squirtgun.

Entanglements giant nets.

Esotropic radiator Causes temporary retinal damage. Can be fired from a conventional weapon, an explosive burst superheats a surrounding gaseous plasma and inspires a laser-bright flash.

Flare Grenade Lights up an area of 20m radius to almost daylight and anything further than 20m will be at low light. Available in any color, with or without parachute.

Flare Shells Will light up a diameter of 30m.

Flash-bang This will cause three 1 million candlepower flashes to explode with a huge bang. Will knock down any target for a bit and do little damage to the surroundings.

Flash-bang Shells Similar to flash-bang grenades fire in a triangular pattern from the muzzle of a weapon and ends 25m away where it is 3m wide. Stuns only. Shatters glass within 10m.

Flash Bomb Emits a blinding flash.

Gas chemical Legality dependent on gas employed.

Hallonugen chemical Causes a target to hallucinate.

Information-based weapons Use where targets are highly dependent on information technology.

Infrasound High-powered speakers generate very low frequency sound waves can easily penetrate most buildings and vehicles. Disorients targets and causes vomiting and messes up bowel control.

Irritants Things like tear gas.

K.O. chemical Knocks out target, but comes with the warning that more than 6 hits will stop a target's heart which will result in death.

Lasers Concentrated light which are not harmful to the target's vision but, affects the brain/nerve system. Can put a human being out of action for a short time. Can be mounted on a rifle.

Laser Dazzle Sight (LDS Laser beams to blind targets.

Lifeguard System tracks bullets in flight and projects the bullet flight track. Locates the origin.

Liquid Metal Embrillement (LME dissolves metal vehicles. A target could be tanks and APCs.

Low frequency noise Disorients enemy troops and causes vomiting. Put test animals into a stupor.

Mace To hit the target you need to be 5m away and facing the target.

Magnetic phosbeams gun Affects the retina of the eye. Can make a target groggy and disoriented, as if struck over the head.

Microbes eat engine hoses, belts, electrical insulation.

Microwave weapons Microwaves can alter the blood/brain barrier.

Militech Dart Multi MDM 341 This weapon uses two cartridges of air for delivery of drugs.

Militech Electronics Taser Size of a large flashlight. Fires a bolt of energy up to 10m to hit target.

Militech Taser Can be countered with regular body armor.

Militech Taser II Can deliver 15,000 volts to a target.

Mini Sentry System Can stop vehicles used in terrorist, car-jacking or hostage situations. Generates high energy pulses for the engine controls of the target vehicle which causes the engine to stall. The device can be installed on any vehicle, so it can be triggered at anytime by authorities, at a location of their choosing. Gives no-warning of the loss of power.

Mitsubishi Taser A small pistol and fires a small dart connected by wire to the weapon. Can penetrate some body armor. Shocks the target.

NAUSEA chemical May cause permanent brain damage with repeated hits.

Nelspot "Wombat Paintball gun.

Non-blinding optical munitions or weapons Laser like weapons.

Non-lethal nets Hand-deployed or fired from 37mm or 40mm grenade launchers.

Olfactory agents Chemicals.

Optic weapons Used to temporarily blind the target or put them into a trance or seizure.

Passive imaging Concealed weapons detector without the need for a direct physical search.

Peppa-Spray Made from chili pepper extract similar to mace.

Pepper spray and mace Disables target. A very effective non-deadly force weapon.

Petrochem DRUG-A-THUG Delivers a solid dose of a paralyzing chemical to the target.

Pursuit Security Inc. STUNDART Pistol An over/under break open format pistol that fires a .45 low velocity cartridge. Has two copper prongs on the front to deliver a stun charge.

Pursuit Security Inc. Webgun A rifle like single shot weapon. The "Webber" has a conical muzzle with 4 blast directing nozzles which fire 4 elliptical weights. Between these weights, a spider-web like nylon net which is pulled open by the trajectories of the weights. This snares the target in a fast moving, hard pulling tangle. Web large enough to cover any one person.

Pyrophoric particles Burn out engines when drawn into air intakes;

Retractable spiked barrier strip For stopping fleeing vehicles. The strip can place its spikes in either the active (vertical) or passive (horizontal) positions, allowing law enforcement personnel to lay the unobtrusive-looking strip across a road far in advance of the approach of a fleeing vehicle. No damage occurs to passing vehicles until the spikes are activated, which can be done at some distance.

RFR traditional frequency radiation system Could provide an effective stun capability over a large area. Some potential uses include dealing with terrorist groups, crowd control, controlling breeches of security at military installations, and antipersonnel techniques in tactical warfare.

Road Patriot System Uses a reaction engine powered projectile to position a high energy pulse generator under the suspect vehicle, where the electromagnetic discharges can disable the engine control systems. The system deploys toward the fleeing vehicle.

Road Sentry electronic car stopper system Stops vehicle traveling at high rates of speed.

Rubber bullets Damage or injury can occur to the target. Stuns beyond 3m.

Scatter packs Similar to a non-deadly force claymore mine. Contains 50 rubber pellets capable of stunning target. Must be mounted stationary or on tripod.

SECURES (System for the Effective Control of Urban Environmental Security) Employs acoustic sensors to detect, recognize and pinpoint the location of gunfire.

Silver Shroud vehicle disabling net Deploys against an automobile.

Simpson Dart Rifle An old hunting rifle used to knock out big game for capture.

SJ01-100KSSTUN 100,000 Volt Mini Stun Gun Electronic device that puts out a high voltage shock that can cause muscle spasms and a dazed mental state.

SJ01-100KCSTUN 100,000 Volt Curved Stun Gun Electronic device that puts out a high voltage shock that can cause muscle spasms and a dazed mental state.

SKUNKER Fires a burst of gas or spray up to 2m. Fits in any pocket or bag.

Sleep drug Could stop the target's breathing.

Sleepmax II If this hits the target's bare skin, (or soft armor), then the target gets drowsy and falls asleep.

Slick-em High-viscosity slick chemical.

Smoke grenade Available in any color.

Snare net A personnel entanglement net.

Smoke shells Cover a 3m radius circle with dense smoke, (blocks IR, Thermograph, etc.)

Sonic weapons Used to induce pain. Inaudible, but causes loose bowels, dizziness, and excessive vomiting when aimed at a target.

Spraypaint grenade Explodes to cover target in 20 colors of paint.

Stand-alone scanner Concealed weapons detector.

Stench bomb Uses chemicals to cover an area of 5x5m with a sticky and extremely pungent substance.

Sticky Foam A chemical used to immobilize an individual.

Sticky Net A chemical net used to immobilize an individual.

Stinger grenade Crowd dispersal. A small grenade that causes injury similar to a bee sting or maybe a BB pellet. Can fire wooden batten, rubber pellets and a foam baton with 40-millimeter grenade launchers. Fired at the ground, ricochet off the ground and to hit people in the legs. Can fire 40-millimeter projectiles from a grenade launcher as well as a 12-gauge shotgun.

Sting Ne Employs a high-voltage pulse generator to quickly immobilize armed combatants and other highly dangerous individuals.

Stun guns these will knock out targets.

TTRANQUI-PISTOL Air pistol that can fire a dart of liquid drugs or chemicals.

Tasers fires wires to target 15ft. away, may knock out or disable target.

Black-Zap glove An electrified mesh glove with effects equal to a taser. Powered by an armband power-pack.

Pulse Rifle An EMP rifle, which affects humans and any unshielded electronics, (it shields itself). At close range it can fry electronics and disable people for hours! A tight beam weapon effecting only 1 person or object per shot, (body location fairly irrelevant), but it fires in a corridor so people standing in a line behind the target are effected. Armor has no effect.

Microwaver A microwave weapon to disrupt electronics and cyberware.

Thermal gun Raises target's body temperature to 105 or 107 degrees, thereby simulating a disabling fever.

KEYGUARD Key Chain Sprayer Similar to a penlight or lipstick case with a black enamel finish over solid brass. Disguised. Sprays 10% pepper gas (the most effective) from any position. Can be included in survival kits or for undercover officers if needed.

POCKETGUARD Clip Sprayer 10% disguised pepper gas sprayer. Sprays from any position. Can be included in survival kits or for undercover officers if needed.

PENGUARD Defense Pen Disguised writing, ballpoint pen also contains 10% pepper gas. Refills easily and safely. Sprays from any position. A safety guard prevents accidental discharge. Can be included in survival kits or for undercover officers if needed.

PENGUARD L.E. Deluxe Pen Disguised writing ballpoint pen contains 9 grams of 10% pepper gas. Can be quickly and easily refilled. Sprays from any position. A safety cap completely encloses the sprayer. Can be included in survival kits if needed.

LITEGUARD Palm Light Sprayer Palm-size low profile flashlight has a high intensity krypton bulb powered by a 9 volt battery and disguised 10 grams of 10% pepper gas. Can be refilled and can be fired from any position. A positive safety prevents accidental misfires. Can be included in survival kits or for undercover officers if needed.

PISTOLGUARD Gas Pistol Pistol shaped, balanced, aimable device, constructed of black high impact plastic resin which incorporates both strength and lightness. Fires multiple sprays of 10% pepper gas from a 300 gram replaceable canister. Fires from any position.

LITEGUARD L.E. Flashlight 3 cell flashlight has a high intensity krypton lamp and a replaceable 54 gram canister of 10% pepper gas. Ideal for outdoors. Effective on humans. Fires from any position.

Urban Technology Drug Damage depends on drug in round.

VSI-Visual Stimulus and Illusion Mind Control. Projects a holographic image into the clouds.

WEAPON RANGES

25mm pistol (up to 9mm/.45)	15m
25mm pistol (over 9mm)	50m
25mm launcher	250m
25mm rifle launched (any caliber)	90m
Tsunami 25mm (not hand held)	1500m (hi-pressure grenades)
30mm rifle launched (any caliber)	60m
30mm launcher	230m
30mm hi-pressure	1300m (not hand held)
40mm rifle launcher (any caliber)	30m
40mm launcher	225m
40mm hi-pressure	1600m (not hand held)

www.ingramcontent.com/pod-product-compliance
Lightning Source LLC
Chambersburg PA
CBHW030522290526
45786CB00004B/1571